Another Bungalow

ANOTHER BUNGALOW

MAURA WAY

Press 53
Winston-Salem

Press 53, LLC
PO Box 30314
Winston-Salem, NC 27130

First Edition

Cover design by Kevin Morgan Watson

Cover art, "House Project – Illistration" Copyright © 2013 by Luca Di Filippo, licensed through iStock by Getty Images

Author photo by Martin Tucker

Library of Congress Control Number 2017954777

Printed on acid-free paper
ISBN 978-1-941209-64-6

for 5401 39th Street

Contents

Our Town / 1

Netted Gems / 2

Malocclusion / 3

Ramrod / 5

Out to Lunch / 6

Mnemonic Device / 9

Common Core / 13

Sound Advice / 15

After Dinner at Luigi's / 16

In Mahwah, the Rhododendron / 17

Flowers Big as Houses / 18

Quick Point / 19

He Asks / 20

Vestibule / 22

Trappists / 23

Gilgamesh / 25

That October / 26

Thanksgiving / 27

Lever / 28

Inspection / 29

Keeping Count / 30

Curb Strip / 31

Lupercalia / 32

Decade / 33

Salvage / 34

Belle of the Ball / 35

My Cup Runneth Over / 36

Humor Seeker / 37

Soul Assist / 38

Baffle Gate / 40

Leadlight / 41

At the Diner / 42

A Choosing / 43

Backwards City / 44

Salient / 45

July in Her Eye / 46

For the Benefit of the Flower / 47

New Souths / 48

Modern Warfare / 51

Feedback / 52

Second Acts / 53

Losingly / 54

To Eating Alone / 55

Effete / 57

Vocation / 58

Maundy Thursday / 59

Act of Contrition / 60

Hemmed / 61

Buck Moon / 62

Rinky Dink / 63

Acknowledgments / 67

Author biography / 69

Our Town

The new drama
teacher said we
all had accents.

We said no
we di-ent.

He made us say:
> greasy without the z
> could *have*
> would should *have*

stemming our duhs

cases of the Mundys
concerns 'bout plooshin

Gone

the sweetness of ornch drink
the tang of earl and vinerger

Because then
I noticed
and was
ashamed.

Netted Gems

Pull all the kids off the internet.
Put them out on hot concrete porches.
Give them knives and cantaloupes
to play with. They will know what to do:
hack, scoop, then fling fruit guts
into the moldering azalea bushes.
They will awkwardly separate
sweet from green with needless
knives, when their own mouths
would less dangeroulsy do.
They will stab their rough-hewn
chunks, shove metal toward their
own melony tongues in the most
knuckleheaded of ways. They will
scrape the blade through clenched teeth,
as effortless orange-left glides down them.
They won't think to double-tap like or
Snapchat their decorated faces. They will
never comment, "This is fun," because it is.

Malocclusion

at thirteen, I am fit
for a bite plate—a pretty
pink imitation of the
roof of my mouth

no one can see it, but I can
flip it clack it snap it
and even wear it
swimming in the ocean

until someone tries to dunk
me and, everything is hilarious,
I spit it out in a melodramatic
timely teen laughing jag

I watch my bite plate
disappear into the gray.
I dive after it like it will be
as easy to find as a penny

for years after this day
an aunt or cousin will
point to an odd shell
on the shore and say my

bite plate has finally come
back to me. I will jam many
salty purplish fragments
behind my buck teeth

and smile and nod. I like
thinking of my bite plate
beyond me, out there in
the drink. The thirteen-

year-old roof of my mouth
immortalized in hard
plastic and housing
some strange crab,

invisible plankton colony,
lily roots, or even now
scum-covered at the
bottom of a hog lagoon

gone uncorrected, buried,
laughter ejecting even this
small cry for perfection

Ramrod

She wanted   poker straight ropy rain
point A to point B hair   blunt cut at Harlow's of Washington
for that New York style   taken time to grow

A man she thinks is French is assigned to cut her hair. *No feathers,* she
says. Yes. Yes. *No.* A brown mini-Fawcett bench presses a smile. She
tips well—wanders half a block down Wisconsin Avenue.

Cut it all off. Second stylist asks if she had a haircut recently. *No. Why?*

It was to lie, to have her hair cut twice in an hour. Fifty dollars + another
twenty. They knew—the tiny hairs stuck to her neck, the shocked follicles
and smell of product. On the walk home it car wash rained.

        "Anyone with big eyes and a long neck can wear a pixie cut,"

she reads ten years later. She is spiked,
squinty and chewing on her turtleneck

Out to Lunch

D.C. in those days when I hate
everyone but me—that's tight
pants days—unzipped
friends are saying *send it back* &
figurehead & *folic acid*
& & we're eating outside after
going to see a movie with
an -ing word in the title, usually
the first word, followed by
a name that isn't mine
what a bore

Chris Matthews' wife
is eating here. Kathleen
is wearing toile from
head to toe. She is
on the channel seven
news, but I didn't know
who he was until I got
cable. Looks like she isn't
going to finish her spanikopita.

This gets us on a topic: the lady
talking to me's mom had group
with Diane Rhem, I'm not
supposed to know, that was before,
you know and I know. I watch white hinges
holding together the lippiest of lips
as the story is told. I will inadvertently
walk into the restaurant with my
pants still unzipped when

I go to the bathroom later.
I tell myself to remember
to zip up, but will not.
This not-remembering
must be a decision;
I mourn the time when
underwear exposure was not
expected, when it was
a good enough reason
for a big embarrassment
session in the bathroom
      tempus fugit Beth Smith
      wrote in magic marker on my
      fly when everyone's signed
      jeans for junior high long
      ago size five birthday presents.
      Beth was known for sometimes saying
      things that were not so smart, but after that
      I for one knew she was *but I can't focus on that*
anymore because a woman is on
her earpiece, speaking maybe
Korean. It's not Japanese. The
boys at the table next to us can't
understand her. I can tell.
I know these things.

Five years ago she would
be a crazy woman. This
dainty hand pressed to
a robotic ear, even
with French tips,

wouldn't fly under
these umbrellas.

Usually I'd think, *oh, isn't
it nice to hear people
speaking in all these
languages* but today
it makes me wish

I could understand
blooming everything
—had a beltless
cotton-lined
fugit ingot
G-suit.

Mnemonic Device

1.
Down the basement
the Trinitronic was new.
There the Motown Anniversary Show
was a special special special.
There on the sofa of indoor
outdoor carpet texture—me 11 she 2.
It used to be upstairs
before we needed

           extra bedroom

                Zoe.

My mother chickened
out at the last second
named her Catherine
just in case she turned
out *normal.* Not a medical
condition, just, well, normal.

I wanted to be a Cate—
so I tried to call the baby
that   I also tried to sleep
in the crib. I was 9. Cate
just didn't take.
She was cumbersome:
Catherine Zoe.

So she declared herself
just Zoe in the first grade.
That's when it really matters.

That's when it sticks.
That's when you are most
grateful for a three-letter name.

I was in eighth grade by then
and didn't want to be
a Cate anymore. By then
I wanted to be a girl Ramone.
I'm glad I didn't have
another sister
or a puppy.

Catherine Zoe was
right there next to me
that night on the sofa
she doesn't know
and she doesn't
remember trying
to moonwalk.

2.

so she doesn't remember
I've seen it in the
others   my friends
all youngests

      all my closest   they don't remember
much
about how they got stray marks
or what was in their minds when—
        It's not their minds
they remember pin numbers
and phone numbers
tibia   *tarsus*   *claw*
turn in their taxes
      on time, but—

In eighth grade, two girls   I still know
      made a remembering machine

It was an index card
with a rectangle cut out
of the upper left hand corner.
You could run it down
your vocabulary list or state
capitals and give yourself
a quiz before the quiz.
They named it *Test Ease* ™.
      I thought it was funny
        sounding
and geeky as hell   they didn't.
I laughed at them
said they were perverts

They didn't get it and nothing could quell the excitement.
"Don't you understand? A quiz *before* the quiz?   thought
it might catch on   make them rich.

                        But why feel bad?

Now when
I say, "Remember your *Test Ease* ™?"
They say, "You remember the
                        weirdest stuff."
But somehow
it reminds them of Physics class   see *Hill Street Blue*s
                                carved into my desk

and one of them recites the Greek
alphabet says that was our first
test grade. Then the other joins in unison

                        somewhere around omicron

Common Core

This subway schoolmarm knows one thing:
recertification for teaching job = many binders/dry-erased
central office silk blouse/seat hours and sticky note kind of nights

It's two weeks until Easter but
there're already rabbits on the earrings
and tote bags of these prepared folks.
The one in charge says
from The Smart Board:

Tell the students (repeat after me)
THE CLIMAX IS THE MOST EXCITING PART

pastel fingernail polish fingernail shadow **RIGHT HERE**
double tap and spread with haughty flourish
on the do-not-write-on-this-surface screen

Make them say the climax determines eventual theme. This is text complexity.
Lean into the standards. Do you want to see **my** *system for determining meaning?*
O o o o, principal smiles and we clap a while.
I do one late clap for denouement.

Blue = Theme
> a. Expo markers smell like sadness
> b. run screaming to Fashion Bug manager job
> c. don't you want to show mastery?
> d. just shade the damn circle completely

Red = Text-to-Self Connections
> There is a man driving west,
> traveling at three days away from the woman.

The answer will be expressed in a number
sentence   *reading across the curriculum.*

It's not always so exciting
when the story changes
everything afterward

                                        The End.

Sound Advice

If you find a few sets of realistic and well
made scrubs, you may never have to really
get dressed again. Scrubs also generate
respect in our society! Sadly, this is not
always true of our pajamas. In case of
emergency, shout   *I'm sorry, I'm a
vet. tech*   unless   of course, it is
a cat who is dying—
then run.

After Dinner at Luigi's

I sideswiped a very big Benz
right on Dupont Circle proper.
I was driving my Dodge Neon
and was on a half-blind date
with a law student. He told
me not to say anything. Very
friendly men smoking small
cigarettes poured out of the
Mercedes, took a quick look,
and said it was nothing. *No
damage, see?* Such a sturdy
sand colored luxury sedan
immune to green economy
cars with questionable lane
integrity. My date and I had
met at a Halloween party: he
wasn't in costume, and I was
dressed up as a hockey puck.
When he spilled his Zima at
dinner, I was relieved that the
jinx part of the date was over.
Then I got in the fender bender
on our way to Bedrock Billiards.
I've always assumed the men
in the Benz were Saudis; the
flowy one-piece button-ups,
the white keffiyeh affixed with
twisted black cords. Now I know
this was a hasty generalization.
The law student never called
me again. I beat him at pool,
and surely he imagined unmet
 miracles under that hockey puck.

In Mahwah, the Rhododendron

grow as tall as dogwoods
but no one believes in
New Jersey anymore.
Kilmer's trees and tracks
much more lovely than his
rest stop where I call
from to say I'll be there
soon. Payphone feels as
old as granite. The crisp
pressure of neat squares:
A Job To Do. Each number
issues its own report. Digits
remembered as design;
triangles and crosses.
Go ahead and finger the
cool ribbed snake, speak
into the gray, pick up so
much left by other hands
and mouths. The slick-umed
man in khakis circles but
keeps his distance. This
is to know your limits, your
effect on others. Back home
my rhododendron droop in
humid mulch. They are so
young and disconnected—
never ever having had to
stop to make a phone call.

Flowers Big as Houses

My paper roses no longer hang in grandma's
attic. The house sold to the highest bidder—
china and linen bartered between aunts.
No one claimed my tattered drawings, hidden
among afghans and flatware at the estate sale.
I remembered them too late, scribbling
crayonless, feeling naked as a stick person.

Roses once suspended from rafters by thin strips
of yellow tape. Red swirls on primer paper ignore
lines of rigid blue. Flowers big as houses dwarf
the flimsy figures without hair, flesh, or hands.
Dot noses unable to smell their gargantuan gardens.
My name appears on the horizon:
boldy black and spelled wrong.

These circles overtake me, ruby gyres disturb
lines of time. Supple petals drip from rafters,
collect in reflecting pools, pink around my feet.
The roses drink here from perpetual waters—
still wildly spiraling through my dotted lines.

Quick Point

Thread   the wide-eyed
plastic pink   needle with thick,
licked   and   lumpy blue yarn.

Bebe repeats:

in through the back, go
upstairs, then one next door

In sweet and inscrutable houses

my painted-on   butterfly awaits

but   I   can't   quite   catch   her

small caterpillar fingers
        pull too hard
                snap needles
lose wings behind

                          this airy canvas

He Asks

Which arm are you going to offer a dog if it attacks you?

He picks up a bag of potatoes in the produce aisle,
looks at me for the answer. I don't understand this
kind of taking care, but every time I answer
    Left.

  (so I can punch him with my good hand)

Back home, there were D.C. words for punching:
    stole "He stole him in the face"
    glass "She just walked up and glassed him"
    slide "He got a slider— fell back twenty feet"
       mostly performed upside-the-head.

I got out of all my fights by not making my presence known. In 7th
grade, a big girl didn't want me and Alexa Schatzow changing up in
her locker room because we were so *fugly and nasty*. I agreed and took
a D in P.E. My gym uniform said Rodriguez in magic marker on the
front, under the Viking. I bought it used for two bucks off a 9th
grader. *Rodriguez, say you're fugly and nasty. . .*

I, Rodriguez, am fugly and nasty.

   He continues with the bear drill.

Pushing the shopping cart I repeat:
I'm to get under the vehicle.

  And don't try to help me, got it?

Yes.

I, Rodriguez, will watch shoelaces, asphalt,
and paws while you are mauled to death. *Yes.*

I imagine blacktop, but I am from a city.
I suppose a bear attack would take place
on dirt. And why does he think the truck
would be so nearby? Why wouldn't
we just both get in the truck and drive away?
This quiz takes place in the frozen food
aisle. My hands are full of 39-cent burritos.

Give him plenty of room.
Resist the urge to run.

Vestibule

There is a school where
when you walk in
they don't try to kill you.
No, this isn't about
that; it's much slower.

Trappists

we are monks and
have a lot of work
we need to get done
just stop talking
stop talking so
you can shut up
we remember you
from second grade
you and Oliver didn't
have to write *I will*
not talk in class 100
times and he didn't
even know English
but you did
we remember
that kind of thing

Oliver we can understand
he was wearing wooden
shoes for crying out loud
but we still resent
you—you more sneaky
than quiet and knowing
our language so well

if you had to write it
would have stuck
you wouldn't be
annoying us monks
who are just trying
to make jelly! Our

products are available
at Whole Foods all over
the Mid-Atlantic region.
(this is so much better)

Maybe even you have heard of us?

Gilgamesh

should have stayed a tyrant. Enkidu
free. I never found my comfort zone &
so I wildly loaf as a spindly substitute.
The full bravado of trees astounds me.
They never had to learn to use a cup
or wrestle. My instincts have followed
me. What comes easily ought to be denied
if you fashion yourself some kind of hero.

That October

the leaves hung on,
barnacle stubborn,
to keep an obstructed
view. Clear November
waits for the dentist,
legs crossed, looking at
an old *Parents* magazine.
It seems like everyone
else is called back so
quickly! He worries that
his breath is becoming
sour. He hopes he gets the
voluptuous hygienist again.

Thanksgiving

the everything bagel repeats, stick tree
after stick tree, biggest traffic days
replete with speed traps and rage

/a muffled life through
automatic windows/
inside: to go limp is
an action to survive

O, yellow diggers on the shoulder bright and strong,
I was surely meant to commandeer you:
pull certain levers, make important holes!
Yellow diggers with only a driver's seat—
sweet windowless yellow diggers;

this shotgun could kill me.

Lever

The fever broke;
it's just one of the ways I show
love. Everything I eat is poison,
but I stay in line, getting better,
and better with the old human
mandible. I need a name for my
attitude; it's not good. It pivots,
but you've taken a load off.
Arms can also be a
fulcrum of support.

Inspection

They research school systems, crime,
taxes, upcoming road projects, the
the airport's noise cone. They are
aware of the danger of being blinded
by the glitter of cosmetic features.

They look for horizontal
cracks (bulges and
deflections may
indicate serious
structural problems)

They are wary of a home where there is evidence
of deferred maintenance. They test underground
tanks for integrity. Look for signs of water
extrusion. Suggest X-ray evaluations of
surfaces painted prior to 1978

and they marry
for love.

Keeping Count

The furniture is moving. Don't thank anyone
for lunch more than once. Unfortunately, the
lower falls will never lead to the upper falls.
I tend to donate the furniture back to where

I got it in the first place. I'm self-centered. I
went to visit my living room on display at
the Idaho Youth Ranch Thrift Store before
I left town forever. I sat right down on my
spot on the sofa and checked out a defunct
karaoke machine displayed on a shelf. Out
of habit, I tucked my hand between the arm
and cushion and found my own turquoise
mala beads. This was not the first time I

shoplifted. Maybe I should have let them
go? They were supposed to grant me
serenity and manifest a true path in life.
I'm not sure those are things I should
think about. I want the future to affect
the past. I want to treat you to a falafel.

Curb Strip

What makes me look
away? The stern intensity
of the pooping dog shake
or the wild-haired sad sack
behind him about to wave
a grocery bag mittened hand?
He thinks he must know me.
I look really familiar to him.

Lupercalia

Gray silences stick to your
ribs: there are four-leaf plants

along the ribbons of highways
that you can't see. Snow's sterile

curse will not be shaken off by
nudity, revelry, thongs of goat.

Subtle strings make obedience
seem kind. Oh, it can be, if you

listen. May I dance? Is that a flute?
Free spirit must be a euphemism,

but I've lost track of the other side.
A barren panic blankets auspicious

hills and dales. Just good, they say.
No one calls their kids trapped souls.

Decade

In this town without a river, I landed
myself, wondered what would become of me.
Bungalows were easy to take for granted
flanked by early oranging river birch trees.
In this place, I could call myself mother.
Wide porch boards sounded so satisfying,
but like a sofa under a dust-cover
it was noisy and only looked relaxing.
Nothing could ever stain that upholstery.
I made the mortgage payment and complex
stews. I was called names, said rosaries,
conjuring only hexes and the sweats.
Yeah, I hear the damn train whistle beckon:
hopped off a box car right here, I reckon.

Salvage

You just can't see it. Nothing but glum
pots and wet blankets behind rusty
barbed wire fences, used by impotent
old men, long dead. You'll think you
need to understand this pile because
to the dog, his junkyard is beautiful.
Without the yard, he is just dog.
Without the junk, he is ordinary.
Without you, he thinks he has nothing to
guard against. His busted sofa cushions
suddenly become busted sofa cushions.
No more shadows of lost pillowy love
or endless clouds of innards from his
dreams of instinct. He will die to protect
this. Don't cry when you can't understand
the ways of junkyard dogs. They have
nothing you need. Let sleeping dogs bark
away their tapeworms and mulligrubs alone.

Belle of the Ball

Silk bluebells never open, forced or not
always buds, these California ladies.
Far better from afar, like the foothills' dry tops
where slick crickets mate in a shadeless Hades.
Only long shots grant cool, purple quiescence.
Distance dissembles the views, flowers, girls:
our synthetic desert obsolescence.
Mustachioed, tenacious woolly blue curls,
slough off Vaseline bulbs and lampshade scarves
while magic hour makes wormsmeat of us all.
Standing water kills the desert bloom. Varves
resurrect our stories. The belle of the ball
is sediment, silt, the wrinkled and rooted.
What is left is the beauty that denudes us.

My Cup Runneth Over

Like so many variegated leaves, I begin to become
all one color instead. The rest of life is not as
exciting as the day you win the lottery. I want a second
career. They are calling it Red October. It is the 9th.
It is 92 degrees. My druthers have cooled.
I don't know what to do with all this love.
My shepherd's pie days are over. There's something
about me that is cold as stone. But oh, how the children
do love me! The children with small, expensive hearts.

Humour Seeker

This is the day (this is the day) that the Quakers make me bring
a handmade gift and my mock liver pâté to the holiday party. Most

other Friends School teachers seem to be involved in a cottage industry.
They knit complex hats, hand-dip candles, make America's top pies. I melt

a record, attach it to a copper pipe and call it a Rockin' Robin
Birdbath. It's so Catholic. There are others like me, but not here.

I am red-cheeked and corpulent, optimistic and irresponsible. My inner
light longs to rip on your inner light without worrying about your feelings.

Your light's so dim it takes it two hours to watch 60 Minutes. Like that.
My pâté tastes perfunctory. I'm not saying I'm sanguine, but

I can't deny the liver much longer.

Soul Assist

Here we make tree
balls. Chicken wire
spheres wrapped in
lights, thrown in
branches, attached
to fly fishing line
and stubborn orange
extension cords. A
canopy of wild light
hangs high above
our boxy houses.
There is something
very insistent inside
that compels us to
eat the fat, suck the
bones, and light up
the night, light up the
night, for God's sake,
light up the night *right
now*, lest we all
fall down, one by
one and together. *Hush
hush*, the tree balls say,
*these oaks will bloom
again*. Here, where
looking an azalea in the
face will make you laugh
out loud and the noisy
green of spring burns
phosphorescent, we band
together and work extra

hard to convince ourselves
it will all come back again.
Yes, the tree balls say, *from
these same skinny sticks, from
these blank and sorrowful skies.*

Baffle Gate

Last day of the year: eyes are going
balls are falling. Still with tinsel, we'll
make merry coronas, laurels, glee
garlands. This year I will ski. Good
old dogs will die for auld lang syne.
Getting my hair done at Chakras Salon
costs two hundred bones. My party should
not trust me. I nearly read *A Tale of Two Cities*
while getting a pedicure. Be careful what
you get good at doing because you'll end
up doing it forever. The snow turned into
rain. I can recline; I seem very relaxed.

Leadlight

snow days are no days   here
with only Zelda. That's what I named
a squiggly quavering of light that
sometimes appeared in my childhood
bedroom through the 1911 windowpane.
I hadn't seen her in fifteen years, but
she followed me to another bungalow
just when I needed her because everyone
is outside playing with their kids and dogs
in the snow. I like to make things fun for
people. So does Zelda, waving to me in
the midday light I so rarely get to enjoy.
I put on my most exciting underwear
and wonder what's to become of me.

At the Diner

Salami sandwich, hold the mayo,
stares at me from a heavy plate.
He is so cold and unforgiving.
Oh, it is my heart; it is my heart.
Oh, for a nice bowl of ripe tomatoes.

A Choosing

Wasn't until recently—
I found out the word
hadn't always been
tiger.   I too
        plant marigolds
holler America.

Backwards City

The dream bagels beat the biscuits
twice before we awoke to bogo offers

from above. Turns out it was just buy
one get one 50% off, but we didn't know

that back then. I thought I could teach
them to follow, to bust up the clean

platter club and unsweet the tea. But here
I am beached, bemyrtled, and nowhere

near how it used to be. This is a dalrymple
in time, a surprise, a lovely rock agape, an

electrical socket that works, a gay dolphin
that's gone home to interpret other signs.

Salient

The man got out
of his green Miata

and walked briskly
with a long heirloom

watermelon under his arm,
the Bradford, the sweetest.

Zucchini was soon turned
into spaghetti noodles,

squash blossomed & I knew
all about it from television.

Freeman High School
wants the rebel mascot

back, but Nat Turner
is not an option under

consideration. Balmy
Battle of the Crater

summer, can't stay
in trenches forever.

July in Her Eye

100s of high mucketymuck
tomatoes burst like so many
mouths in mouths. Loud yellow
birds shit from branches of hot
pink trees. All are welcome to make
garish messes   * here *   during me.

For the Benefit of the Flower

Overspent rosebuds
complain about the
lack of some sordid
seed recognition. Once,
we yearned to earn the
sad, righteous thorns
that would make
us beautifuler.

The young still
can see our prickly
wisdom. They are poised
to listen to sirs and
ma'ams who will not
speak. Who are so far
away and forever busy,
fertilizing inflatable
flower costumes.

New Souths

Let hate and prejudice have no place
here on granite fountains sponsored
by the Serendipity Garden Club. You
can build all the parks you want but
what you need are people who would
rather be outside than inside, adults who
can stand being around other adults who
they have not hand-selected for freshness
and quality. Other adults with other
habits. Those other unpredictable adults
who dream, and strive, and love.

*

A single kid swings listlessly on a seven
thousand dollar cedar custom-designed
play set in his massive backyard.
His trees are too new for shade. He
drags his foot. He doesn't have
to share. He goes inside to
play *Doom* for the rest
of the afternoon. He's very
good at it. He hasn't had
the same opportunities as
other American boys.

*

I'm sitting on a bird! I'm flying!
the children in the downtown
swingless park scream at sullen
strangers. They are in danger
down here. They have made
something out of nothing. This
world has not been childproofed.
Dogs die. The wolf wins.

*

There is a Gathering Place at the
new urbanist shopping center where
you can safely loose the kids. Yes.
This is the best of all worlds! They
can run and play and eat ice cream.
It looks so safe, ensconced by high
end retail and little white lights,
lots of security guards. It's just
like being in a city but without,
you know, so it's better.

*

Five boys on small bikes skid
through the park disrespecting
the granite. Some are too small
to be out on their own. Someone
should be watching them. They
jump the curb into traffic, laughing
and screaming because they are
alive. They may die early. They
may not want to work in a cubicle
or on a screen all day. They haven't
had the same opportunities
as other American boys.

*

Indoor cats don't miss the outside
because they don't know it exists.
Just because I thought *catch
a tiger by the toe* was the
only version of the rhyme
doesn't mean it was.

How will the children
know what to change if we
don't let them see our
problems ? Oh, but they
see, oh say, can they see.

They see the
backward past
and it is us.

Modern Warfare

Her perennials are mounding; primrose,
salvia, and the man's, inside, online.
His call of duty never ends. Heroes
must be made and levels climbed:
die, then come back, a quantum entanglement.
Levers get pulled and bodies hit the floor.
The earth is safe: his wife digs decadent
holes for overloved succulents, soapwort,
coralbells. Her peonies will start slow
but may last a century. She crushes each
ant between petals; speaks to the yarrow.
Deft hands find dandelions and lay siege.
Achilles knew flowers can staunch real wounds,
but only in small arenas they bloom.

Feedback

There's difficulty in click
bait. Jon Heder's head, the
center of Mesmer's swirls;
too many allusions and click
heres for thinking. This is how
you change your life these days,
fast. My disk has slipped—I've
jumped the demographic
broom. The hurlyburly's done
and my nose is large. I can't
understand these spells when
Moneypenny gadgets all came
true—no use in swooning
over cameras in pens no more.
"No, I can't live chat, join
your community. For I don't
believe in blinking things
the promise of customizing,"
my profile winked. "Options
are an end game," the
hedge-pig whined.

Second Acts

A done marriage's very persnickety
history can entrap with a fly paper
that's long lost its stick. This soliloquy
cements me in empty amphitheaters
that are still real ruins. Countenances
trail ribbons tied neatly behind human
heads. Why can't I get out of this boundless
bow? My guffaw is mucilage; movement
binds me tighter. Only two catharses
are available, and one will break my
compound eye beyond belief, but Pegasus
must be bitten, and who would hurt a fly?
So I fall back to earth, wings and sight intact.
That show is over. I stand to be unmasked.

Losingly

Laurels rested on others'
heads. Satiation is found
out beyond the bronze.
Lagniappe is the dream

after destiny breaks. Not
winning, but still sublime.
An exoglorious smile, a
silent shine   just steps

below the dais. We sing
no odes to the charmed
lives of fourth place or
tries. We don't have to.

No lionizing soapbox is
necessary to understand
the tumescence of small
but generative victories:

skipped stones, hard found
lakes, the knots that finally
became expertly tied and
saved us all from drowning.

To Eating Alone

Once I felt so awkward around you:
twenty-two years old looking for
an apartment and wanting to sit
down in air-conditioning to eat chana
masala in Fredericksburg, the very first
tandoor oven in town. You were there
for me then, and I had a newspaper.
I loved you right away even though
I seemed afraid. You were a milestone
thirteen years later while I waited for
the divorce to be final. Then your
complicated Pho was so demanding!
Thankfully, it was all I could do.
Your red plastic basket of greens
was so festive that I could even
look at the bulbous eyes of the
tanked fish and not be afraid.
Those times were excruciating
and also beautiful. But now I can
have you without all this trepidation.
Looking forward to you makes
shopping malls worth it! You are
my first stop on federal holidays
or early dismissals for snow. I
recommend you to anyone who
will listen. I know you will make
me lonely one day—but not now.

Few are Chosen

The pilgrims are invited to be part of the episode.
Fat monks will watch over your teeny structure.
Cutting your hair, taking off your clothes: these
will mark your crossing from one phase to another.
Or you could change your name. I miss being
Catholic. Like after you turn 30, you can't dream
of being a prodigy anymore: I liked waiting to be
one of those miracle girls. Oh, my heroes were
so full of martyrdom. Bernadette, Clara Barton,
Mary McLeod Bethune, Elizabeth Seton. Work
horses all. Vital people vitalize, the sages say. I
am degenerate and questless. Hot only to trot.

Effete

I wonder what Lady GaGa is doing for her birthday? I wonder if she can get excited about life when her hair is greasy? I can't even get up the enthusiasm to wash it. It's boring in the shower. If it were my party, I would invite Amy Sedaris; that would cheer me up. She could have a craft station or make grilled cheese. I would be too tired to plan anything. I know I should be grateful to make thousands of dollars a year, but I have been a schoolteacher for twenty years, and it's usurping my spirit, plus I have no idea if I'm doing it right. Just look at what's happening now. Plus, everyone keeps passing me by. It's nice to wave. There: I feel better. It's a parade! As I get older, I'll bring a lawn chair and a red-white-and-blue afghan.

Vocation

Not speaking fills my inbox, stained glass
sentinels are beautiful but only minusculely
transparent. Certain times of day are better
than others. Hands were made for talking
and the Lyceum has a dazzling new voice:
teach with your mouth shut and you'll
patronize no one. The silent disco makes me
dervish, but I'll give it a whirl. No one voice
can speak for the e pluribus unum but you
might as well try. The red reflections on the
wall have gone bone blank. It is scary to go
to church at night when the windows look
like blackboards. I have low expectations.

Maundy Thursday

When the mandate was eradicated,
the women soaked their feet and
sighed. They knew it was coming.
There would be no hair to blot
their toes, but still the water did
rejuvenate their soles, a refuge
from the standing, leaning, and
campaigning. Striving keeps you
on and makes you hate the journey.
My mother told me to protect my
knees. She has two new ones. I
was disgusted when my father took
off his shoes in church, but it was
part of the mass, so I had to be
rational about it. Tomorrow you
can kiss a crucifix, but for today
try to be joyful in your service.

Act of Contrition

There used to be a red
light that clicked on
when a confession

was in session. I used to stare
at it while waiting in the pew,
dreading the green. Today

I saw stock footage of this very
church, Blessed Sacrament, in
Religulous on Netflix. Another

time, while in my own living room,
I saw my estranged ex-husband live
streaming: he was in an establishing

shot of a high school gym just beyond
Paul Giamatti's head. I recognized the
way he stood in the bleachers in a blazer

waving a rolled up newspaper. A pantomime
of a familiar screaming about an imaginary
wrestling match behind a forgiving screen.

Hemmed

Vacillation sandwiched between small
suns, rusted belts, always bibles. Regions
of great glee if you acknowledge their exits.
This-or-That Lane Boutique has been in business
since Prohibition, but most people already have a
house full of antiques. The day the car finally
died we sat on the trunk alongside the highway
until a cousin happened by in a functioning vehicle.
We had wallets full of photos and cash tender. It
was a broken axle. It was before cellular. It wasn't
worth fixing. We called the wrecker once we got back
to the house. Ambivalence was not for us, we believed.

Buck Moon

My antlers came in. The half-
way point of the summer reeks
of botched casseroles. I saw an
artichoke fully blooming. Pain
bored a hole in my forehead &
luckily something came out. I
cannot afford to hunker. Eating
everything in sight, I shed my
only velvet. It's been a year, but
I didn't spar enough to make a
difference. I liked the soft pedicles
even if they weren't going to get
me anywhere. In the garden, I can
smell the woman and her pungent
kitchen. Next year I'll leave antlers
in the oak forest for the rabbits to
gnaw. Her garden will be gone.
Not all of us are made for this
life; eating flowers before they
even jackpot, perfecting the rut.

Rinky Dink

for Anthony Myers

There's a conduit on roller
skates named me. The disco
ball is my heart, and I am tall.
Every step the children take is
a miracle and would bulge old
discs. Round and round is all
there is and that's okay for a
change. Oh, how this going
nowhere exhilarates me. No
labyrinth, no moguls, just the
swerve and the music. I win
absurd contests. I change
direction. There is relief
without finish lines. Here,
you just run out of time.

The author would like to thank the editors of the journals and magazines where the following poems first appeared, sometimes in a slightly different form or under the name Maura Payne:

Aubade, "Flowers Big as Houses"
Beloit Poetry Journal, "He Asks"
Burnside Review, "Keeping Count"
The Chattahoochee Review, "Malocclusion"
DIAGRAM, "Few are Chosen" and "Leadlight"
Drunken Boat, "Belle of the Ball"
Fredericksburg Literary Arts Review, "Inspection"
MARGIE, "Our Town"
O.Henry Magazine, "Quick Point" and "Soul Assist"
The Ocean State Review, "Lupercalia"
Verse, "A Choosing," "At the Diner," "Feedback" "For the Benefit of the Flower," "In Mahwah the Rhododendron," "July in Her Eye," "Lever," "My Cup Runneth Over," "Thanksgiving," "That October," and "Vestibule"

"Flowers Big as Houses," "Quick Point," and "Rinky Dink" were published as broadsides for *Poetry in Plain Sight*, a community poetry project by Winston-Salem Writers.

Acknowlegments

I would like to thank all of my teachers, especially my parents, for noticing I was a poet before I did. Mrs. Whitley, Mrs. Jackson, and Mrs. Euston at Murch Elementary and Mrs. McCullough at Deal Junior High all inspired and demanded intelligent creative expression. "The Seedling" by Paul Laurence Dunbar still echoes through my brain. These hardworking women made me write, and they made me memorize poetry. And that has made all the difference. At Mary Washington, Connie Smith taught me how to read, enjoy, and remember poems I never would have come to on my own because I thought they were old and boring. They were not. Later, at Boise State, Janet Holmes challenged me to be both rigorous and experimental in both my poetry and scholarly pursuits. Along with Karena Youtz, Mark Brown, Matt Reiter, and Kenneth Koch, she taught me octopus language.

Over twenty years as an educator, my students have always been my best teachers. Some are thirteen, some aren't with us anymore, and some are pushing forty. . . I hope I have given as much as I have received. Being in the classroom is the best professional development seminar or writing workshop I've ever attended.

Thank you to the people of Summit School and New Garden Friends School for supporting the arts and artists of all ages. Summit Soul Food and the studio program inspired and encouraged me to share my work publicly after a long dry spell. Summit helped me travel to conferences and work with fellow writers/educators, including young people and Frank Morelli. Also, I am forever grateful to NGFS for awarding me a creative writing teacher sabbatical. Several poems in this book began in 2011 while I was back in Idaho, thanks to the program.

To all the McAllisters, Paynes, and Ways, my siblings, aunts, uncles, cousins, nieces, nephews, first cousins once-removed, in-laws, and play-cousins, thanks for being a source of constant support and material. I don't know what I would do without my boisterous extended family "getting me." When you're so clearly not from around here in North Carolina, it's wonderful to be able to come home to such a welcoming and joyous tribe of children, oddballs, accountants, readers, unicyclists, innovators, teachers, mug designers, and sit-down comedians.

I have endless gratitude and love for my mom and dad, Mary Lou and Robert. Latin teachers by trade, they are the original word nerds, the keepers of the bungalow, the milk of human kindness. Anyone who has stopped by their porch or parlor has learned a lesson in the power of warmth, inclusivity, and perhaps even direct object pronouns. For my mother, every day is a poem. She dares to eat peaches. How could I not become a poet?

Thanks to Kevin Morgan Watson and Press 53 for supporting me and so many other writers and poetry-lovers in North Carolina and beyond. Discussing publication in the Reynolds High School library under the oil-painted eyes of decades of school principals was truly epic. I'm not sure they approved.

And although Mark would rather I say nothing, he is my set-point and my hero. One of these days, I might even write a poem about him.

Maura Way was born and raised in Washington, D.C. Her poems have been featured in numerous magazines and journals including *Verse*, *Beloit Poetry Journal*, *Drunken Boat*, *DIAGRAM*, and *The Chattahoochee Review*. She has been a teacher for over twenty years, most recently at Summit School and New Garden Friends. Maura lives in a yellow brick bungalow in Greensboro, North Carolina, with her husband Mark.

CPSIA information can be obtained
at www.ICGtesting.com
Printed in the USA
BVOW03s0251311017
499015BV00003B/212/P